Gorillas live near the
equator in the jungles
of Africa.

Gorillas are the largest apes.
They are almost 6 feet tall and
are very, very strong.

The gorilla is really a kind,
peaceful animal.

Gorillas become very angry if
they are bothered.

Gorillas are vegetarians. This
means they eat fruit and
wild plants.

Every night, a gorilla makes
a bed out of leaves
and branches.

Gorillas live in peaceful, happy families. There are often 5 to 15 in the family.

Gorillas don't like water very much.

Adult male gorillas are much bigger than females and often weigh twice as much.

It takes baby gorillas several months to learn to walk. Mother gorilla carries her baby in her arms or on her back.